Exploring the Holy Bible: A Guide for Non-Christian Seekers

Isla M. Alves

Introduction

Welcome to this book, a resource designed to help you deepen your understanding and appreciation of the teachings found in the New Testament of the Bible. In this guide, we will explore the purpose and methodology of sentence block diagramming, a valuable tool for studying and comprehending the Scriptures.

Understanding the structure and meaning of sentences is essential for grasping the messages conveyed in the New Testament. Sentence block diagramming provides a systematic approach to break down sentences into their constituent parts, allowing for a more in-depth analysis of the text. We will introduce the concept and guide you through the process of block sentence diagramming, enabling you to engage with the biblical text on a deeper level.

The format of sentence block diagrams will be outlined, providing you with a clear and organized way to present and analyze the structure of sentences. By following this format, you will be able to create your own sentence block diagrams and gain insights into the connections and relationships within the text.

To put your newfound knowledge into practice, we will provide examples of sentence block diagrams from selected passages in the New Testament. These examples will serve as practical illustrations of how sentence block diagramming can enhance your understanding and interpretation of the Scriptures.

Furthermore, we will provide an outline of specific books from the New Testament, such as the First and Second Letters of Paul to the Corinthians. These outlines will serve as a roadmap, guiding you through the key themes and teachings contained within these biblical texts.

As you embark on your journey through the New Testament, we encourage you to engage in thoughtful reflection and study. Allow the words and teachings of the Scriptures to inspire and challenge you, and use the tools and techniques presented in this guide to delve deeper into their meaning and significance.

Remember that this guide is meant to be a friendly companion on your spiritual journey. Approach the New Testament with an open heart and a desire to grow in your faith. May this guide serve as a helpful resource as you explore the rich wisdom and timeless truths found within the pages of the New Testament.

The
New Testament
of Our Lord and Saviour
Jesus Christ

TRANSLATED OUT OF THE ORIGINAL GREEK:
AND WITH THE FORMER TRANSLATIONS
DILIGENTLY COMPARED AND REVISED
BY HIS MAJESTY'S SPECIAL COMMAND

Authorized
King James Version

Contents

Purpose of Sentence Block Diagramming

The beauty of this Sentence Block Diagram is that you see everything visually **in one glance**. Right away, it is very easy for you to isolate important themes of Bible Books.

Why is it important for us to grasp the key themes of each book of the Bible?

Our minds are usually not very focused because we are distracted by many daily matters. So when it comes to reading the Bible and doing our devotions, it is very difficult to put our minds in focus. Words are just words and they don't' speak to us. And when I started showing people my Bible with Sentence Block Diagram, they get very excited because they see everything in one flash. Suddenly the words in the Bible become meaningful to them because of the format.

Suddenly what seems to be so difficult to understand is suddenly made easy. They discover that they are able to isolate key themes in their Bible studies preparation and sermon passages.

I discover that my congregation remembers the sermons and Bible studies much better. What they remember, they will continue to meditate on their own, and they grow spiritually.

Bible Study Method: Sentence Block Diagram

Learn how to study the Bible by using this analytical approach of using sentence block diagramming method.

1. This approach is the path to a deep understanding of the major themes of each book of the Holy Bible.

2. The entire Sentence Block Diagramming is to isolate the nouns, the verbs, the prepositions, adjectives, object, adverbs etc so that you can see the Bible verses written in a 'visual' format.

3. You will be able to see the main theme - the subject matter - clearly when the sentences are blocked and marked in different lines.

4. Most of our Bibles are formatted in either by verses or by paragraphs. In this Sentence Block Diagram, you will see sentences broken off in segments so that you can see the major themes and parallelism.

5. You can use this as a Bible study guide to help you prepare sermons, Bible lectures, Bible seminars, Bible study groups for adults, Bible study group for youths. You can also use this approach to teach Sunday School.

6. To do sentence block diagram method, you need to know your English grammar a bit so that you can isolate Subject and Predicate. The Subject is the main noun and the predicate is the main verb. You can actually pick up an English Grammar Book and see how they parse sentences to subject and predicate forms.

How to do Block Sentence Diagramming?

It is very easy.
Follow these simple rules.

Rules:

1. **Find the SUBJECT of the sentence.** A sentence at the very least must have a subject. The subject can be a noun or pronoun (he, she it, etc). It is usually at the beginning. The subject is usually a person, or persons, or things that perform an action, or actions.

2. **Find the Predicate.** The predicate is the main verb. Usually it follows the main noun. Verbs are words that show actions. For eg. show, dance, walk, run, write, draw. Some verbs are state of being when they use 'to be'. For eg. Am, is, are, was were, etc.

3. **Find the Direct Object.** This is the person or thing that receives the action of the verb.

4. **The remaining words are modifiers** in the sentence serve to describe, clarify or give us more information about the subject or the verb.

a. Adjectives usually describe the noun.

b. Adverbs describe the action.

c. Prepositional phrases are groups of words that begin with a preposition and end with a noun or pronoun. They function the same way as an adjective or an adverb.

5. **Write the sentences out in diagrams form.** A diagram arranges the parts of a sentence like a picture in order to show the relationship of the words within the sentence.

Since this is an ebook, I am unable to provide all the horizontal, vertical and slash lines.

I will simply place them below the words. You will be able to see where they are placed when you read them.

Sentence Block Diagram Format

1. By doing sentence diagramming of each book, I am able to extract the major themes the author wants to tell us without subjective interpretation.

2. When you see the format of the sentence diagram, you will see everything clearly in ONE flash.

3. You will also discover that you can't do without this formatting each time when you prepare a sermon or a Bible study.

4. When all the points are laid out so clearly in front of you, you can extract 10 to 15 sermons from the points and sub points. This will give you a series to preach at church for 3 months to half a year.

5. You will be able to do expository preaching to feed your congregation weekly without running out of material.

6. For each sermon, you have a very vivid THEME to preach on.

7. The main theme of the sentences starts at the left hand margin so that you can see where the main clause begins.

7. All the other sub points are indented.

8. Sometimes with the indention, you see alphabetical points or number points – they are all sub points to help you see the structure.

9. All the sentence diagramming is done in an easy-to-read for your meditation and study.

10. The major of the work is done for you by giving you the VISUAL format.

Read the Bible in Sentence Block Diagram

In this series of Books, I have done all the hard work for you by giving you the result of the 'Sentence Block Diagram'. You do not need to struggle through to do the sentence block diagram yourself. **You can start reading the Bible in the Sentence Block Diagram Method by having these sets of Bible Books.**

In order not to do any interpretation for you, I don't tell you how to section your sermons or Bible study material. I've tried to avoid any interpretation and that is the reason why I am not including an outline of each book for you. For the outlines of Books, you can get them anywhere on the net.

This is a non-conventional method of Bible studies. It is to make the whole book in 'block sentence diagrams' so that you can absorb the major themes using this visual method.

1. Once you know the focus of each section, you can easily compile your own Bible Study notes.

2. You don't need to depend on Bible study outlines done by others. You would know the right questions to ask and discover the answers yourself through meditative studies.

3. When you see the final lay out of the sentence block diagram, you will have ready made at least 10 thematic sermons to preach with insights & great content.

4. Block diagramming is a useful technique for studying the Bible that allows one to carefully and precisely study the meaning of the text. It is not fool-proof, yet, it is reliable and helpful because it forces the reader to make conscious decisions concerning the meaning of the text. All too often, we read the Bible without really understanding what is said, or worse yet, we do not even attempt to

struggle with the issues involved in discovering precisely what God's Word says. Block diagramming forces the reader to struggle with the text -- this is the goal.

I wish you happy learning. I've laid out the whole book in sentence diagramming with grammatical structure and point form analysis. The entire Book of the Bible is in block sentence diagram form. This will give you a powerful visual effect to read the Bible.

May the Word of God enlighten our souls and strengthen us and those around us with God's eternal light.

Raymond & Rosa Suen
Dec 2013

Holy Land With RR

Outline of The First Letter of Paul to the Corinthians

1. Introduction (1:1–9)

2. Problems in the Church (1:10-4:21)
    1. Division (1-4)
    2. Immorality (5)
    3. Lawsuits (6:1-11)
    4. Prostitution (6:12-20)
    5. Sexual Relationships (5-7)
    6. Idolatry (8-10)
    7. Women & Worship (11)
    8. Communion (11)
    9. Spiritual Gifts (12-14)
    10. Death & Resurrection (15-16)

3. Conclusion (16:10-24)

1 Corinthian Chapter 1

Paul,
  called to be an apostle of Jesus Christ
  through the will of God,
and
   our brother
Sosthenes,

to the assembly of God
  which is at Corinth;
    those who are sanctified in Christ Jesus,
    called to be saints,
     with all who call on the name of our Lord Jesus Christ in every
place,
      both theirs and ours:

Grace
to you
and
peace
  from God our Father and
    the Lord Jesus Christ.

I always thank my God concerning you,
  for the grace of God
    which was given you
     in Christ Jesus;

  that
  in everything you were enriched in him,

in all speech   and
  all knowledge;

1Co 1:6

even as
the testimony of Christ was confirmed in you:

1Co 1:7

  so that you come behind in no gift;
    waiting for the revelation of our Lord Jesus Christ;

1Co 1:8

  who will also confirm you until the end,
    blameless in the day of our Lord Jesus Christ.

1Co 1:9

God is faithful,
  through whom you were called
  into the fellowship of his Son,
            Jesus Christ,
            our Lord.

1Co 1:10

  Now
I beg you,
  brothers,
  through the name of our Lord,
            Jesus Christ,
1. that you all speak the same thing   and
2. that there be no divisions among you,   but
3. that you be perfected together
    in the same mind   and
    in the same judgment.

1Co 1:11

  For
it has been reported to me
  concerning you,
        my brothers,
  by those who are from Chloe's household,

that
there are contentions among you.

1Co 1:12

Now
I mean this,
that each one of you says,
a. "I follow Paul,"
b. "I follow Apollos,"
c. "I follow Cephas,"   and,
d. "I follow Christ."

1Co 1:13

Q1. Is Christ divided?
Q2. Was Paul crucified for you?   Or
Q3. were you baptized into the name of Paul?

1Co 1:14

I thank God
that
I baptized none of you,
   except Crispus and Gaius,

1Co 1:15

so that
no one should say that I had baptized you into my own name.

1Co 1:16

(I also baptized the household of Stephanas;
besides them,
I don't know whether I baptized any other.)

1Co 1:17

For
Christ sent me
   {1} not to baptize,
   {2} but to preach the Good News
      -- not in wisdom of words,
      so that the cross of Christ wouldn't be made void.

1Co 1:18

For
the word of the cross
  1. is foolishness to those who are dying,
    but
  2. to us who are saved it is the power of God.

1Co 1:19

   For it is written,
  "I will destroy the wisdom of the wise,
  I will bring the discernment of the discerning to nothing."
      [Isaiah 29:14]

1Co 1:20

Q1. Where is the wise?
Q2. Where is the scribe?
Q3. Where is the lawyer of this world?
Q4. Hasn't God made foolish the wisdom of this world?

1Co 1:21

  For seeing that
     in the wisdom of God,
A. the world
  through its wisdom
 didn't know God,
B. it was God's good pleasure
  through the foolishness of the preaching
    to save those who believe.

1Co 1:22

For
Jews ask for signs,
Greeks seek after wisdom,

1Co 1:23

but
we preach Christ crucified;
  a stumbling block to Jews,   and
  foolishness to Greeks,

1Co 1:24

but
  to those who are called,
    both Jews and Greeks,
Christ is   a. the power of God   and
        b. the wisdom of God.

1Co 1:25

Because
the foolishness of God is wiser than men,   and
the weakness of God is stronger than men.

1Co 1:26

  For you see
your calling,
    brothers,
that
  1. not many are wise   according to the flesh,
  2. not many mighty,   and
  3. not many noble;

1Co 1:27

but
A. God chose the foolish things of the world
  that
  he might put to shame those who are wise.
B. God chose the weak things of the world,
  that
  he might put to shame the things that are strong;

1Co 1:28

and
C. God chose the lowly things of the world,   and
        the things that are despised,   and
        the things that are not,
  that
  he might bring to nothing the things that are:

1Co 1:29

  that

no flesh should boast (a) before God.

1Co 1:30

But (b) of him,
    you are in Christ Jesus,
  who was made to us
    (1) wisdom from God, and
    (2) righteousness   and
    (3) sanctification,   and
    (4) redemption:

1Co 1:31

  that,
    according as it is written,
  "He who boasts,
  let him boast in the Lord."   [Jeremiah 9:24]

1 Corinthian Chapter 2

When I came to you,
    brothers,
I didn't come with excellence of speech   or
              of wisdom,
    proclaiming to you the testimony of God.

  For
I determined not to know anything among you,
  except   (1) Jesus Christ,   and
        (2) him crucified.

  I was with you
    a. in weakness,
    b. in fear,   and
    c. in much trembling.

My speech and my preaching were
  1. not in persuasive words of human wisdom,
  but
  2. in demonstration of the Spirit and of power,

that
your faith wouldn't stand
  1. in the wisdom of men,
  but
  2. in the power of God.

We speak wisdom,
    however,
  among those who are full grown;

yet
a wisdom
  1. not of this world,
  2. nor of the rulers of this world,
    who are coming to nothing.

1Co 2:7

  But
we speak God's wisdom in a mystery,
   the wisdom that has been hidden,
  which God foreordained before the worlds
    for our glory,

1Co 2:8

  which none of the rulers of this world has known.
   For
  had they known it,
  they wouldn't have crucified the Lord of glory.

1Co 2:9

  But as it is written,
   "Things which an eye didn't see,   and
         an ear didn't hear,
     which didn't enter into the heart of man,
   these God has prepared for those who love him."
       [Isaiah 64:4]

1Co 2:10

  But
  to us,
God revealed them
 through the Spirit.
 For
 the Spirit searches all things,
       yes,
       the deep things of God.

1Co 2:11

For who among men knows the things of a man,

except the spirit of the man,
    which is in him?
Even so,
no one knows the things of God,
  except God's Spirit.

1Co 2:12

But
we received,
  a. not the spirit of the world,
  but
  b. the Spirit which is from God,
that
(1) we might know the things that were freely given to us by God.

1Co 2:13

(2) Which things also
we speak,
  not in words which man's wisdom teaches,
  but which the Holy Spirit teaches,
    comparing spiritual things with spiritual things.

1Co 2:14

Now
the natural man
  1. doesn't receive the things of God's Spirit,
    for they are foolishness to him,
  and
  2. he can't know them,
    because they are spiritually discerned.

1Co 2:15

But
he who is spiritual discerns all things,
  and
he himself is judged by no one.

1Co 2:16

"For who has known the mind of the Lord,

that he should instruct him?" [Isaiah 40:13]
But
we have Christ's mind.

1 Corinthian Chapter 3

1Co 3:1

Brothers,
I couldn't speak to you
  a. as to spiritual,
    but
  b1. as to fleshly,
  b2. as to babies in Christ.

1Co 3:2

I fed you
 with milk,
 not with meat;
for you weren't yet ready.
  Indeed,
  not even now are you ready,

1Co 3:3

  for
  you are still fleshly.
   For insofar as there is
   1. jealousy,
   2. strife,   and
   3. factions among you,
  Q1. aren't you fleshly,   and
  Q2. don't you walk in the ways of men?

1Co 3:4

  Q3. For
  when one says, "I follow Paul,"   and
  another,   "I follow Apollos,"
  aren't you fleshly?

1Co 3:5

  Q4. Who then is Apollos,   and
    who is Paul,

but
servants through whom you believed;
and
each as the Lord gave to him?

1Co 3:6

a1 I planted.
a2 Apollos watered.
    But
a3 God gave the increase.

1Co 3:7

So then
b1 neither he who plants is anything,
b2 nor he who waters,
    but
b3 God who gives the increase.

1Co 3:8

Now
C1 he who plants   and
C2 he who waters are the same,
    but
c3 each will receive his own reward
    according to his own labor.

1Co 3:9

For
we are God's fellow workers.
You are   God's farming,
        God's building.

1Co 3:10

According to the grace of God
    which was given to me,
  as a wise master builder
I laid a foundation,
and
another builds on it.

But
let each man be careful how he builds on it.

1Co 3:11

For no one can lay any other foundation
  than that which has been laid,
    which is Jesus Christ.

1Co 3:12

But if anyone builds on the foundation
  with a. gold,
    b. silver,
    c. costly stones,
    d. wood,
    e. hay,   or
    f. stubble;

1Co 3:13

each man's work will be revealed.
  For
  the Day will declare it,
    because it is revealed in fire;
    and
    the fire itself will test what sort of work each man's work is.

1Co 3:14

If any man's work remains which he built on it,
he will receive a reward.

1Co 3:15

If any man's work is burned,
he will suffer loss,
  but
  he himself will be saved,
    but as through fire.

1Co 3:16

Q1: Don't you know that you are a temple of God,
    and
Q2: that God's Spirit lives in you?

A. If anyone destroys the temple of God,
God will destroy him;
  for God's temple is holy,
    which you are.

Let no one deceive himself.
B. If anyone thinks that he is wise among you in this world,
let him become a fool,
that he may become wise.

  For the wisdom of this world is foolishness with God.
    For it is written,
  "He has taken the wise in their craftiness."   [Job 5:13]

  And again,
  "The Lord knows the reasoning of the wise,
    that it is worthless."   [Psalm 94:11]

  Therefore
let no one boast in men.
  For
  all things are yours,

  1. whether Paul,
  2. or Apollos,
  3. or Cephas,
  4. or the world,
  5. or life,
  6. or death,
  7. or things present,
  8. or things to come.
  All are yours,

and
you are Christ's,
and
Christ is God's.

1 Corinthian Chapter 4

So
let a man think of us
  as Christ's servants,
    and
    stewards of God's mysteries.

  Here,
    moreover,
    it is required of stewards,
    that
    they be found faithful.

  But with me
it is a very small thing that I should be (1) judged by you,
    or (2) by man's judgment.
      Yes,
  I don't judge my own self.

  For I know nothing against myself.
    Yet I am not justified by this,
      but he who judges me is the Lord.

Therefore
judge nothing before the time,
    until the Lord comes,
      who will both
        (1) bring to light the hidden things of darkness,
          and
        (2) reveal the counsels of the hearts.
      Then

each man will get his praise from God.

1Co 4:6

Now these things,
  brothers,
I have in a figure transferred to myself and Apollos
    for your sakes,
that
  in us
you might learn not to think beyond the things which are written,
  that
  none of you be puffed up against one another.

1Co 4:7

Q1. For who makes you different?
Q2. And what do you have that you didn't receive?
  But if you did receive it,
Q3. why do you boast as if you had not received it?

1Co 4:8

You are already filled.
You have already become rich.
You have come to reign without us.
    Yes,
  and
I wish that you did reign,
  that we also might reign with you.

1Co 4:9

For,
I think that God has displayed us,
  the apostles,
    last of all,
  like men sentenced to death.
For
we are made a spectacle to the world,
  both to angels and men.

1Co 4:10

A. We are fools for Christ's sake,
   but you are wise in Christ.
B. We are weak,
   but you are strong.
C. You have honor,
   but we have dishonor.

1Co 4:11

   Even to this present hour
we 1. hunger,
   2. thirst,
   3. are naked,
   4. are beaten,   and
   5. have no certain dwelling place.

1Co 4:12

A. We toil,
   working with our own hands.
B.   When people curse us,
   we bless.
C.   Being persecuted,
   we endure.

1Co 4:13

D.   Being defamed,
   we entreat.
E.   We are made as (a) the filth of the world,
   (b) the dirt wiped off by all,
       even until now.

1Co 4:14

I don't write these things
   a. to shame you,
   b. but to admonish you
       as my beloved children.

1Co 4:15

   For
   though you have (a) ten thousand tutors in Christ,

yet (b) not many fathers.
For
  in Christ Jesus,
I became your father
  through the Good News.

1Co 4:16

I beg you   therefore,
be imitators of me.

1Co 4:17

  Because of this
I have sent Timothy to you,
  who is my beloved and faithful child in the Lord,
  who will remind you of my ways
        which are in Christ,
        even as I teach everywhere in every assembly.

1Co 4:18

  Now
some are puffed up,
  as though I were not coming to you.

1Co 4:19

  But
I will come to you shortly,
    if the Lord is willing.
And
I will know,
  (a) not the word of those who are puffed up,
  (b) but the power.

1Co 4:20

  For
the Kingdom of God is {1} not in word,
but {2} in power.

1Co 4:21

What do you want?
Shall I come to you

a. with a rod,
  or
b. in love and a spirit of gentleness?

1 Corinthian Chapter 5

   It is actually reported that
there is sexual immorality among you,
      and
      such sexual immorality as is not even named among the Gentiles,
that
one has his father's wife.

You are (1) puffed up,
   and
(2) didn't rather mourn,
   that
   he who had done this deed might be removed from among you.

   For
I   most certainly,
      as being absent in body
      but present in spirit,
have already,
      as though I were present,
judged him
   who has done this thing.

   In the name of our Lord Jesus Christ,
you being gathered together,
and
my spirit,
   with the power of our Lord Jesus Christ,

are to deliver such a one to Satan
      for the destruction of the flesh,

that
the spirit may be saved
in the day of the Lord Jesus.

1Co 5:6

Your boasting is not good.
Don't you know that a little yeast leavens the whole lump?

1Co 5:7

Purge out the old yeast,
  that
  you may be a new lump,
    even as you are unleavened.
  For indeed
Christ,
  our Passover,
has been sacrificed in our place.

1Co 5:8

  Therefore
let us keep the feast,
    a. not with old yeast,
    b. neither with the yeast of malice and wickedness,
    but
    c. with the unleavened bread of sincerity and truth.

1Co 5:9

  I wrote to you in my letter
to have no company with (1) sexual sinners;

1Co 5:10

    yet not at all meaning with the sexual sinners of this world,
(2) or with the covetous and extortioners,
(3) or with idolaters;
    for then you would have to leave the world.

1Co 5:11

  But as it is,
I wrote to you
[A] not to associate with anyone who is called a brother

(1) who is a sexual sinner,
(2) or covetous,
(3) or an idolater,
(4) or a slanderer,
(5) or a drunkard,
(6) or an extortioner.
[B] Don't even eat with such a person.

1Co 5:12

For what have I to do with also judging those who are outside?
Don't you judge those who are within?

1Co 5:13

But   those who are outside,
God judges.
"Put away the wicked man from among yourselves."
[Deuteronomy 17:7; 19:19; 21:21; 22:21; 24:7]

1 Corinthian Chapter 6

1Co 6:1

Dare any of you,
   having a matter against his neighbor,
go to law
  before the unrighteous,
  and
  not before the saints?

1Co 6:2

Q1 Don't you know that the saints will judge the world?
Q2 And if the world is judged by you,
   are you unworthy to judge the smallest matters?

1Co 6:3

Q3 Don't you know that we will judge angels?
Q4 How much more,
   things that pertain to this life?

1Co 6:4

  If then,
  you have to judge things pertaining to this life,
Q5 do you set them to judge who are of no account in the assembly?

1Co 6:5

  I say this to move you to shame.
Q6 Isn't there even one wise man among you
   who would be able to decide between his brothers?

1Co 6:6

  But
brother goes to law with brother,
   and
   that before unbelievers!

1Co 6:7

  Therefore

it is already altogether a defect in you,
  that
  you have lawsuits one with another.
Q1 Why not rather be wronged?
Q2 Why not rather be defrauded?

1Co 6:8

No,
but you yourselves
  (a) do wrong, and
  (b) defraud,
  and
  that against your brothers.

1Co 6:9

Q3 Or don't you know that
  1. the unrighteous will not inherit the Kingdom of God?
  Don't be deceived.
  2. Neither the sexually immoral,
  3. nor idolaters,
  4. nor adulterers,
  5. nor male prostitutes,
  6. nor homosexuals,

1Co 6:10

  7. nor thieves,
  8. nor covetous,
  9. nor drunkards,
  10. nor slanderers,
  11. nor extortioners,
    will inherit the Kingdom of God.

1Co 6:11

  Such were some of you,
but
a. you were washed.
b. But you were sanctified.
c. But you were justified

in the name of the Lord Jesus,
  and
in the Spirit of our God.

1Co 6:12

"All things are lawful for me," but not all things are expedient.
"All things are lawful for me," but I will not be brought under the
power of anything.

1Co 6:13

"Foods for the belly, and the belly for foods,"   but
God will bring to nothing both it and them.
But
A. the body is (a) not for sexual immorality,   but
       (b) for the Lord;
  and
B. the Lord for the body.

1Co 6:14

Now
God raised up the Lord,
  and
 will also raise us up
    by his power.

1Co 6:15

Q1 Don't you know that your bodies are members of Christ?
Q2 Shall I then (a) take the members of Christ, and
   (b) make them members of a prostitute?
May it never be!

1Co 6:16

Q3 Or don't you know that he who is joined to a prostitute is one
body?
  For,
 "The two,"
      says he,
 "will become one flesh."   [Genesis 2:24]

1Co 6:17

But
he who is joined to the Lord is one spirit.

1Co 6:18

Flee sexual immorality!
  "Every sin that a man does is outside the body,"
  but
  he who commits sexual immorality sins against his own body.

1Co 6:19

Q4 Or don't you know that your body is a temple of the Holy Spirit
       which is in you,
       which you have from God?
You are not your own,

1Co 6:20

  for you were bought with a price.
Therefore
glorify God   in your body   and
           in your spirit,
                which are God's.

1 Corinthian Chapter 7

1Co 7:1

Now **concerning the things about which you wrote to me**:
it is good for a man not to touch a woman.

1Co 7:2

But,
  because of sexual immoralities,
let each man have his own wife,
and
let each woman have her own husband.

1Co 7:3

Let the husband render to his wife the affection owed her,
and
likewise also the wife to her husband.

1Co 7:4

The wife doesn't have authority over her own body,
but the husband.
Likewise also the husband doesn't have authority over his own body,
but the wife.

1Co 7:5

Don't deprive one another,
  unless it is by consent for a season,
that
you (1) may give yourselves to fasting and prayer,
      and
    (2) may be together again,
      that
      Satan doesn't tempt you
        because of your lack of self-control.

1Co 7:6

But this
I say

by way of concession,
not of commandment.

1Co 7:7

Yet
I wish that all men were like me.
However each man has his own gift from God,
one of this kind,   and
another of that kind.

1Co 7:8

But
[A] I say to the unmarried and to widows,
it is good for them if they remain even as I am.

1Co 7:9

But if they don't have self-control,
let them marry.
For
it's better to marry than to burn.

1Co 7:10

[B] But to the married I command
-- not I, but the Lord --
a. that the wife not leave her husband

1Co 7:11

(but if she departs,
let her 1. remain unmarried,
or else
2. be reconciled to her husband),
and
b. that the husband not leave his wife.

1Co 7:12

[C] But to the rest I -- not the Lord -- say,
a. if any brother has an unbelieving wife,
and
she is content to live with him,
let him not leave her.

b. The woman who has an unbelieving husband,
   and
   he is content to live with her,
  let her not leave her husband.

For
the unbelieving husband is sanctified in the wife,
and
the unbelieving wife is sanctified in the husband.
  Otherwise your children would be unclean,
  but now they are holy.

Yet if the unbeliever departs,
let there be separation.
The brother or the sister is not under bondage in such cases,
but **God has called us in peace**.

  For
how do you know,
  wife,
  whether you will save your husband?
Or
how do you know,
  husband,
  whether you will save your wife?

Only,
  as the Lord has distributed to each man,
  as God has called each,
  so
let him walk.
  So I command in all the assemblies.

Q1 Was anyone called having been circumcised?
  Let him not become uncircumcised.
Q2 Has anyone been called in uncircumcision?
  Let him not be circumcised.

1Co 7:19

Circumcision is nothing, and uncircumcision is nothing,
but
the keeping of the commandments of God.

1Co 7:20

Let each man stay in that calling in which he was called.

1Co 7:21

Were you called being a bondservant?
Don't let that bother you,
but if you get an opportunity to become free,
use it.

1Co 7:22

  For
A. he
  who was called in the Lord
    being a bondservant
  is the Lord's free man.
  Likewise
B. he
  who was called being free
  is Christ's bondservant.

1Co 7:23

You were bought with a price.
Don't become bondservants of men.

1Co 7:24

  Brothers,
let each man,
  in whatever condition he was called,
stay in that condition with God.

1Co 7:25

Now
concerning virgins,
I have no commandment from the Lord,
but
I give my judgment
  as one who has obtained mercy from the Lord to be trustworthy.
1Co 7:26

I think
  that it is good therefore,
    because of the distress that is on us,
that
it is good for a man to be as he is.
1Co 7:27

Q1. Are you bound to a wife?
  Don't seek to be freed.
Q2. Are you free from a wife?
  Don't seek a wife.
1Co 7:28

  But if you marry,   you have not sinned.
  If a virgin marries, she has not sinned.
  Yet such will have oppression in the flesh,
    and
    I want to spare you.
1Co 7:29

  But I say this,
  brothers:
the time is short,
that
    from now on,
1. both those who have wives may be as though they had none;
1Co 7:30

  and
2. those who weep, as though they didn't weep;
  and

40

3. those who rejoice, as though they didn't rejoice;
   and
4. those who buy, as though they didn't possess;

1Co 7:31

   and
5. those who use the world, as not using it to the fullest.
For
the mode of this world passes away.

1Co 7:32

   But
I desire to have you to be free from cares.
A. He who is unmarried
   is concerned for the things of the Lord,
     how he may please the Lord;

1Co 7:33

   but
B. he who is married
   is concerned about the things of the world,
     how he may please his wife.

1Co 7:34

There is also a difference between a wife and a virgin.
C. The unmarried woman cares about the things of the Lord,
   that
   she may be holy both in body and in spirit.
But
D. she who is married cares about the things of the world
   -- how she may please her husband.

1Co 7:35

This I say for your own profit;
   not that I may ensnare you,
   but for that which is appropriate,   and
that
you may attend to the Lord without distraction.

1Co 7:36

But
A. if any man thinks that he is behaving inappropriately toward his
virgin,
   if she is past the flower of her age,   and
   if need so requires,
  let him do what he desires.
  He doesn't sin.
  Let them marry.

1Co 7:37

But
B. he who stands steadfast in his heart,
  having no necessity,
  but has power over his own heart,
   to keep his own virgin,
 does well.

1Co 7:38

 So then
both he who gives his own virgin in marriage does well,
and he who doesn't give her in marriage does better.

1Co 7:39

A wife is bound by law for as long as her husband lives;
 but
 if the husband is dead,
 she is free to be married to whoever she desires,
  only in the Lord.

1Co 7:40

But
she is happier if she stays as she is,
 in my judgment,
 and
 I think that I also have God's Spirit.

1 Corinthian Chapter 8

1Co 8:1

Now **concerning things sacrificed to idols**:
We know
that
we all have knowledge.
  Knowledge puffs up,
  but love builds up.

1Co 8:2

  But
if anyone thinks that he knows anything,
he doesn't yet know as he ought to know.

1Co 8:3

  But
if anyone loves God,
the same is known by him.

1Co 8:4

Therefore concerning the eating of things sacrificed to idols,
we know
  (1) that no idol is anything in the world,   and
  (2) that there is no other God but one.

1Co 8:5

For though there are things that are called "gods,"
  whether in the heavens or on earth;
    as there are many "gods" and
        many "lords;"

1Co 8:6

 yet
  to us
there is
A. one God, the Father,
  of whom are all things,

and we for him;
and
B. one Lord, Jesus Christ,
   through whom are all things,
   and we live through him.

1Co 8:7

 However,
that knowledge isn't in all men.
 But
some,
   with consciousness of the idol until now,
eat as of a thing sacrificed to an idol,
and
their conscience,
   being weak,
is defiled.

1Co 8:8

 But
food will not commend us to God.
 For neither,
1. if we don't eat, are we the worse;
 nor,
2. if we eat,   are we the better.

1Co 8:9

But be careful
 that   by no means does
 this liberty of yours
   become a stumbling block to the weak.

1Co 8:10

For
if a man sees you
   who have knowledge
sitting in an idol's temple,
won't his conscience,

if he is weak,
be emboldened to eat things sacrificed to idols?

1Co 8:11

And
  through your knowledge,
he who is weak perishes,
  the brother for whose sake Christ died.

1Co 8:12

Thus,
sinning against the brothers,
and
wounding their conscience
  when it is weak,
you sin against Christ.

1Co 8:13

Therefore,
  if food causes my brother to stumble,
I will eat no meat forevermore,
that
I don't cause my brother to stumble.

1 Corinthian Chapter 9

1Co 9:1

Q1 Am I not free?
Q2 Am I not an apostle?
Q3 Haven't I seen Jesus Christ, our Lord?
Q4 Aren't you my work in the Lord?

1Co 9:2

If to others I am not an apostle,
yet at least I am to you;
  for
  you are the seal of my apostleship in the Lord.

1Co 9:3

My defense to those who examine me is this.

1Co 9:4

Q1. Have we no right to eat and to drink?

1Co 9:5

Q2 Have we no right to take along a wife who is a believer,
    even as the rest of the apostles,
    and the brothers of the Lord,
    and Cephas?

1Co 9:6

Q3. Or have only Barnabas and I no right to not work?

1Co 9:7

Q4. What soldier ever serves at his own expense?
Q5. Who plants a vineyard, and doesn't eat of its fruit?
Q6. Or who feeds a flock, and doesn't drink from the flock's milk?

1Co 9:8

Q7. Do I speak these things according to the ways of men?
Q8. Or doesn't the law also say the same thing?

1Co 9:9

    For it is written in the law of Moses,
    "You shall not muzzle an ox while it treads out the grain."

[Deuteronomy 25:4]
Q9. Is it for the oxen that God cares,

1Co 9:10

or does he say it assuredly for our sake?
  Yes,
it was written for our sake,
    because he who plows ought to plow in hope,
    and he who threshes in hope should partake of his hope.

1Co 9:11

If we sowed to you spiritual things,
Q10. is it a great thing if we reap your fleshly things?

1Co 9:12

If others partake of this right over you,
Q11. don't we yet more?
  Nevertheless
we did not use this right,
  but
we bear all things,
that
we may cause no hindrance to the Good News of Christ.

1Co 9:13

Q12. Don't you know that
  a. those who serve around sacred things eat from the things of the temple,
    and
  b. those who wait on the altar have their portion with the altar?

1Co 9:14

Even so
the Lord ordained that those
    who proclaim the Good News
  should live from the Good News.

1Co 9:15

But I have used none of these things,
  and

47

I don't write these things that it may be done so in my case;
  for
  I would rather die,
    than that anyone should make my boasting void.

1Co 9:16

A. For if I preach the Good News,
    I have nothing to boast about;
    for necessity is laid on me;
but
B.   woe is to me,
  if I don't preach the Good News.

1Co 9:17

  For
C. if I do this of my own will,
    I have a reward.
But
D. if not of my own will,
    I have a stewardship entrusted to me.

1Co 9:18

What then is my reward?
That,
  when I preach the Good News,
I may present the Good News of Christ without charge,
  so as not to abuse my authority in the Good News.

1Co 9:19

  For though I was free from all,
I brought myself under bondage to all,
that
I might gain the more.

1Co 9:20

1. To the Jews   I became as a Jew,
   that I might gain Jews;
2. to those who are under the law,   as under the law,
   that I might gain those who are under the law;

3. to those who are without law,   as without law
   (not being without law toward God, but under law toward Christ),
   that I might win those who are without law.

4. To the weak   I became as weak,
   that I might gain the weak.
I have become all things to all men,
   that I may by all means save some.

Now
I do this for the sake of the Good News,
that
I may be a joint partaker of it.

Don't you know that those who run in a race
  1. all run,
  2. but one receives the prize?
Run like that,
that
you may win.

Every man
    who strives in the games
exercises self-control in all things.
  Now
they do it to receive a corruptible crown,
but we an incorruptible.

A. I therefore run like that,
  as not uncertainly.
B. I fight like that,
  as not beating the air,

but I beat my body and bring it into submission,
 lest by any means,
 after I have preached to others,
  I myself should be rejected.

1 Corinthian Chapter 10

1Co 10:1

Now
I would not have you ignorant,
  brothers,
that our fathers
  1. were
    a. all under the cloud,   and
    b. all passed through the sea;

1Co 10:2

  and
  2. were all baptized into Moses (a) in the cloud and (b) in the sea;

1Co 10:3

  and
  3a. all ate the same spiritual food;   and

1Co 10:4

  3b. all drank the same spiritual drink.
    For
    they drank of a spiritual rock that followed them,
      and the rock was Christ.

1Co 10:5

However
  with most of them,
God was not well pleased,
  for they were overthrown in the wilderness.

1Co 10:6

Now
these things were our examples,
  to the intent we should not
    1. lust after evil things,
      as they also lusted.

1Co 10:7

2. Neither be idolaters,
   as some of them were.
   As it is written,
      "The people sat down to eat and drink,
      and rose up to play."   [Exodus 32:6]

                                                        1Co 10:8

3. Neither let us commit sexual immorality,
   as some of them committed,
      and in one day twenty-three thousand fell.

                                                        1Co 10:9

4. Neither let us test the Lord,
   as some of them tested,
      and perished by the serpents.

                                                        1Co 10:10

5. Neither grumble,
   as some of them also grumbled,
      and perished by the destroyer.

                                                        1Co 10:11

Now
all these things happened to them by way of example,
and
they were written for our admonition,
   on whom the ends of the ages have come.

                                                        1Co 10:12

 Therefore
let him
   who thinks he stands
be careful
that
he doesn't fall.

                                                        1Co 10:13

No temptation has taken you
   except what is common to man.
God is faithful,

who will not allow you to be tempted above what you are able,
but
  will with the temptation
also make the way of escape,
that
you may be able to endure it.

1Co 10:14

  Therefore,
  my beloved,
flee from idolatry.

1Co 10:15

  I speak as to wise men.
Judge what I say.

1Co 10:16

Q1. The cup of blessing
  which we bless,
 isn't it a sharing of the blood of Christ?
Q2. The bread
  which we break,
 isn't it a sharing of the body of Christ?

1Co 10:17

  Because
there is one loaf of bread,
we,
  who are many,
are one body;
for
we all partake of the one loaf of bread.

1Co 10:18

Consider Israel   according to the flesh.
Q1 Don't those who eat the sacrifices participate in the altar?

1Co 10:19

  What am I saying then?
Q2 That a thing sacrificed to idols is anything,

or
  that an idol is anything?

1Co 10:20

But I say that
  1. the things which the Gentiles sacrifice,
  they sacrifice
    a. to demons,   and
    b. not to God,
 and
  2. I don't desire that you would have fellowship with demons.

1Co 10:21

  3. You can't both drink the cup of the Lord and the cup of demons.
  4. You can't both partake of the table of the Lord,
  and of the table of demons.

1Co 10:22

Or do we provoke the Lord to jealousy?
Are we stronger than he?

1Co 10:23

"All things are lawful for me," but not all things are profitable.
"All things are lawful for me," but not all things build up.

1Co 10:24

Let no one seek his own,
but
each one   his neighbor's good.

1Co 10:25

1.   Whatever is sold in the butcher shop,
eat,
  asking no question for the sake of conscience,

1Co 10:26

  for
    "the earth is the Lord's,
    and its fullness."   [Psalm 24:1]

1Co 10:27

But

2. if one of those who don't believe invites you to a meal,   and
      you are inclined to go,
eat
      whatever is set before you,
    asking no questions for the sake of conscience.

1Co 10:28

But
3. if anyone says to you, "This was offered to idols,"
don't eat it
    for the sake of the one who told you,   and
    for the sake of conscience.
    For
      "the earth is the Lord's,
      and all its fullness."

1Co 10:29

Conscience,
      I say,
    a. not your own,   but
    b. the other's conscience.
For why is my liberty judged by another conscience?

1Co 10:30

If I partake with thankfulness,
why am I denounced for that for which I give thanks?

1Co 10:31

Whether therefore you
    eat,   or
    drink, or
    whatever you do,
do all to the glory of God.

1Co 10:32

Give no occasions for stumbling,
    either
    to Jews,   or
    to Greeks,   or

to the assembly of God;

1Co 10:33

even as
I also please all men in all things,
  a. not seeking my own profit,
  b. but the profit of the many,
that
they may be saved.

1 Corinthian Chapter 11

1Co 11:1

Be imitators of me,
  even as
I also am of Christ.

1Co 11:2

  Now I praise you,
  brothers,
  that
you (1) remember me in all things,   and
    (2) hold firm the traditions,
      even as
      I delivered them to you.

1Co 11:3

  But
I would have you know
that
1. the head of every man is Christ,
  and
2. the head of the woman is the man,
  and
3. the head of Christ is God.

1Co 11:4

Every man praying or prophesying,
  having his head covered,
  dishonors his head.

1Co 11:5

But every woman praying or prophesying
  with her head unveiled
    dishonors her head.
    For it is one and the same thing as if she were shaved.

1Co 11:6

For if a woman is not covered,
  let her also be shorn.
    But if it is shameful for a woman to be shorn or shaved,
    let her be covered.

1Co 11:7

For a man indeed ought not to have his head covered,
because
he is the image and glory of God,
  but
the woman is the glory of the man.

1Co 11:8

For
a. man is not from woman,
  but woman from man;

1Co 11:9

for
b. neither was man created for the woman,
  but woman for the man.

1Co 11:10

For this cause
the woman ought to have authority on her head,
  because of the angels.

1Co 11:11

Nevertheless,
neither is the woman independent of the man,
nor the man independent of the woman,
  in the Lord.

1Co 11:12

For
  as woman came from man,
  so a man also comes through a woman;
but **all things are from God**.

1Co 11:13

Judge for yourselves.

Q1. Is it appropriate that a woman pray to God unveiled?

1Co 11:14

Q2. Doesn't even nature itself teach you
  that
    if a man has long hair,
  it is a dishonor to him?

1Co 11:15

  But
    if a woman has long hair,
  it is a glory to her,
   for her hair is given to her for a covering.

1Co 11:16

But
  if any man seems to be contentious,
we have no such custom,
neither do God's assemblies.

1Co 11:17

But in giving you this command,
 I don't praise you,
 that
 you come together not for the better but for the worse.

1Co 11:18

For
  first of all,
 when you come together in the assembly,
(a) I hear that divisions exist among you,
 and
(b) I partly believe it.

1Co 11:19

 For there also must be factions among you,
 that
 those who are approved may be revealed among you.

1Co 11:20

When therefore you assemble yourselves together,

it is not the Lord's supper that you eat.

1Co 11:21

  For
    in your eating
each one takes his own supper first.
One is hungry,   and
another is drunken.

1Co 11:22

What,
Q1 don't you have houses to eat and to drink in?
Q2 Or do you despise God's assembly,   and
    put them to shame who don't have?
  What shall I tell you?
Q3 Shall I praise you?
  In this I don't praise you.

1Co 11:23

For
I received from the Lord
that which also I delivered to you,
that
A. the Lord Jesus
   on the night
      in which he was betrayed
took bread.

1Co 11:24

  When he had given thanks,
he broke it,
and
said, "Take, eat.
  This is my body,
    which is broken for you.
  Do this in memory of me."

1Co 11:25

  In the same way

B. he also took the cup,
   after supper,
saying, "This cup is the new covenant in my blood.
   Do this,
      as often as you drink,
   in memory of me."

1Co 11:26

For
   as often as
you eat this bread and drink this cup,
you proclaim the Lord's death until he comes.

1Co 11:27

Therefore
whoever
   eats this bread   or
   drinks the Lord's cup
  in a way unworthy of the Lord
will be guilty of the body and the blood of the Lord.

1Co 11:28

But
let a man examine himself,
and
so let him (a) eat of the bread,   and
        (b) drink of the cup.

1Co 11:29

For
he who eats and drinks
  in an unworthy way
    eats and drinks judgment to himself,
      if he doesn't discern the Lord's body.

1Co 11:30

  For this cause
many among you are weak and sickly,
and

not a few sleep.

1Co 11:31

   For
  if we discerned ourselves,
we wouldn't be judged.

1Co 11:32

   But
  when we are judged,
we are punished by the Lord,
that
we may not be condemned with the world.

1Co 11:33

   Therefore,
  my brothers,
  when you come together to eat,
wait for one another.

1Co 11:34

But if anyone is hungry,
  let him eat at home,
   lest your coming together be for judgment.
The rest I will set in order whenever I come.

1 Corinthian Chapter 12

1Co 12:1

Now **concerning spiritual things**,
  brothers,
I don't want you to be ignorant.

1Co 12:2

You know
  that
    when you were heathen [or Gentiles],
  you were led away to those mute idols,
  however you might be led.

1Co 12:3

Therefore
I make known to you
that
  a. no man speaking by God's Spirit says, "Jesus is accursed."
  b. No one can say, "Jesus is Lord," but by the Holy Spirit.

1Co 12:4

  Now
1. there are various kinds of gifts, but the same Spirit.

1Co 12:5

2. There are various kinds of service, and the same Lord.

1Co 12:6

3. There are various kinds of workings, but the same God,
   who works all things in all.

1Co 12:7

  But
  to each one is given the manifestation of the Spirit
    for the profit of all.

1Co 12:8

(1) For to one is given through the Spirit the word of wisdom,
  and

(2) to another the word of knowledge,
     according to the same Spirit;

1Co 12:9

(3) to another faith, by the same Spirit;
  and
(4) to another gifts of healings, by the same Spirit;

1Co 12:10

  and
(5) to another workings of miracles;
  and
(6) to another prophecy;
  and
(7) to another discerning of spirits;
(8) to another different kinds of languages;
  and
(9) to another the interpretation of languages.

1Co 12:11

  But
the one and the same Spirit works all of these,
  distributing to each one separately as he desires.

1Co 12:12

For
  1. as the body
    a. is one,   and
    b. has many members,
  and
  2. all the members of the body,
    a. being many,
    b. are one body;
so also is Christ.

1Co 12:13

For
   in one Spirit
we (a) were all baptized into one body,

whether Jews or Greeks,
  whether bond or free;
and
(b) were all given to drink into one Spirit.

1Co 12:14

For
the body is not one member, but many.

1Co 12:15

  a. If the foot would say,
     "Because I'm not the hand,
     I'm not part of the body,"
   it is not therefore not part of the body.

1Co 12:16

  b. If the ear would say,
     "Because I'm not the eye,
     I'm not part of the body,"
   it's not therefore not part of the body.

1Co 12:17

  c. If the whole body were an eye,
     where would the hearing be?
  d. If the whole were hearing,
     where would the smelling be?

1Co 12:18

  But now
God has set the members,
   each one of them,
in the body,
   just as he desired.

1Co 12:19

If they were all one member,
where would the body be?

1Co 12:20

  But now
they are many members, but one body.

The eye can't tell the hand, "I have no need for you,"
  or again
the head to the feet, "I have no need for you."

No,
  much rather,
those members of the body
  which seem to be weaker
are necessary.

(a) Those parts of the body
    which we think to be less honorable,
on those we bestow more abundant honor;
and
(b) our unpresentable parts
  have more abundant propriety;

  whereas
our presentable parts have no such need.

But
God composed the body together,
  giving more abundant honor to the inferior part,

that
1. there should be no division in the body,
  but that
2. the members should have the same care for one another.

When one member suffers, all the members suffer with it.
Or
when one member is honored, all the members rejoice with it.

Now you are the body of Christ,
and members individually.

1Co 12:28

God has set some in the assembly:
1. first apostles,
2. second prophets,
3. third teachers,
4. then miracle workers,
5. then gifts of
   a. healings,
   b. helps,
   c. governments,
      and
   d. various kinds of languages.

1Co 12:29

Q1 Are all apostles?
Q2 Are all prophets?
Q3 Are all teachers?
Q4 Are all miracle workers?

1Co 12:30

Q5 Do all have gifts of healings?
Q6 Do all speak with various languages?
Q7 Do all interpret?

1Co 12:31

But
earnestly desire the best gifts.
Moreover,
I show a most excellent way to you.

1 Corinthian Chapter 13

1Co 13:1

A. If I speak with the languages of men and of angels,
   but don't have love,
 I have become (a) sounding brass,
   or (b) a clanging cymbal.

1Co 13:2

B. If I have the gift of prophecy,
   and know all mysteries and all knowledge;
   and
 if I have all faith,
    so as to remove mountains,
   but don't have love,
 I am nothing.

1Co 13:3

C. If I dole out all my goods to feed the poor,
   and
 if I give my body to be burned,
   but don't have love,
 it profits me nothing.

1Co 13:4

1. Love is patient   and
2. is kind;
3. love doesn't envy.
4. Love doesn't brag,
5. is not proud,

1Co 13:5

6. doesn't behave itself inappropriately,
7. doesn't seek its own way,
8. is not provoked,
9. takes no account of evil;

1Co 13:6

10. doesn't rejoice in unrighteousness,
11. but rejoices with the truth;

1Co 13:7

12. bears all things,
13. believes all things,
14. hopes all things,
15. endures all things.

1Co 13:8

16. Love never fails.

But
a. where there are prophecies,   they will be done away with.
b. Where there are various languages, they will cease.
c. Where there is knowledge,   it will be done away with.

1Co 13:9

For
we know in part,
and
we prophesy in part;

1Co 13:10

but
when that which is complete has come,
then that which is partial will be done away with.

1Co 13:11

A. When I was a child,
   I spoke as a child,
   I felt as a child,
   I thought as a child.
B. Now that I have become a man,
   I have put away childish things.

1Co 13:12

For
(1) now we see in a mirror,
   dimly,

but then face to face.
(2) Now I know in part,
　　 but then I will know fully,
　　　 even as I was also fully known.

1Co 13:13

But now faith,
　　 hope,　 and
　　 love remain -- these three.
The greatest of these is love.

1 Corinthian Chapter 14

1Co 14:1

Follow after love,
  and
earnestly desire spiritual gifts,
  but especially that you may prophesy.

1Co 14:2

For
[a] he who speaks in another language speaks not to men,
but to God;
  for no one understands;
  but in the Spirit he speaks mysteries.

1Co 14:3

But
[b] he who prophesies speaks to men
  for their
    edification,
    exhortation,   and
    consolation.

1Co 14:4

He who speaks in another language edifies himself,
but he who prophesies edifies the assembly.

1Co 14:5

Now
I desire to have you all speak with other languages,
but rather that you would prophesy.
  For
  he is greater
    who prophesies
  than he
    who speaks with other languages,
   unless he interprets,

that
the assembly may be built up.

1Co 14:6

But now,
brothers,
  if I come to you speaking with other languages,
    what would I profit you,
    unless
    I speak to you either by way
      of revelation,   or
      of knowledge,   or
      of prophesying, or
      of teaching?

1Co 14:7

Even things without life,
  giving a voice,
  whether pipe or harp,
  if they didn't give a distinction in the sounds,
  how would it be known what is piped or harped?

1Co 14:8

For if the trumpet gave an uncertain sound,
who would prepare himself for war?

1Co 14:9

  So also
you,
  unless you uttered by the tongue words easy to understand,
  how would it be known what is spoken?
    For you would be speaking into the air.

1Co 14:10

There are,
   it may be,
so many kinds of sounds in the world,
and
none of them is without meaning.

If then I don't know the meaning of the sound,
  I would be to him who speaks a foreigner,
  and
  he who speaks would be a foreigner to me.

So also
you,
    since you are zealous for spiritual gifts,
seek that you may abound to the building up of the assembly.

  Therefore
let him who speaks in another language pray that he may interpret.

For
if I pray in another language,
  my spirit prays,
  but
  my understanding is unfruitful.

  What is it then?
I will pray with the spirit, and I will pray with the understanding also.
I will sing with the spirit, and I will sing with the understanding also.

  Otherwise
if you bless with the spirit,
  how will he
      who fills the place of the unlearned
  say the "Amen" at your giving of thanks,
  seeing he doesn't know what you say?

  For
you   most certainly
give thanks well,

but the other person is not built up.

1Co 14:18

I thank my God,
I speak with other languages more than you all.

1Co 14:19

However in the assembly
I would rather
(a) speak five words with my understanding,
   that
   I might instruct others also,
(b) than ten thousand words in another language.

1Co 14:20

Brothers,
don't be children in thoughts,
   a. yet in malice be babies,
   b. but in thoughts be mature.

1Co 14:21

In the law
it is written,
   "By men of strange languages   and
   by the lips of strangers
   I will speak to this people.
   Not even thus will they hear me,
      says the Lord."   [Isaiah 28:11-12]

1Co 14:22

Therefore
[1] other languages are for a sign,
   not to those who believe,
   but to the unbelieving;
but
[2] prophesying is for a sign,
   not to the unbelieving,
   but to those who believe.

1Co 14:23

{1} If therefore
the whole assembly is assembled together and
all speak with other languages,
and
unlearned or unbelieving people come in,
  won't they say that you are crazy?

1Co 14:24

{2} But if all prophesy,
and
someone unbelieving or unlearned comes in,
  he is reproved by all,   and
  he is judged by all.

1Co 14:25

  And thus
  the secrets of his heart are revealed.
So he will fall down on his face and worship God,
  declaring that God is among you indeed.

1Co 14:26

What is it then,
 brothers?
When you come together,
each one of you
 1 has a psalm,
 2 has a teaching,
 3 has a revelation,
 4 has another language,
 5 has an interpretation.
Let all things be done to build each other up.

1Co 14:27

A If any man speaks in another language,
  let it be two,
  or at the most three,
   and in turn;
and

75

let one interpret.

1Co 14:28

  But if there is no interpreter,
  let him keep silent in the assembly,
    and
  let him speak to himself, and to God.

1Co 14:29

B Let the prophets speak,
  two or three,
and
let the others discern.

1Co 14:30

  But if a revelation is made to another sitting by,
  let the first keep silent.

1Co 14:31

  For
you all can prophesy one by one,
that
all may learn,   and
all may be exhorted.

1Co 14:32

The spirits of the prophets are subject to the prophets,

1Co 14:33

for
God is
  not a God of confusion,
  but of peace.

As in all the assemblies of the saints,

1Co 14:34

  let your wives keep silent in the assemblies,
    for
    it has not been permitted for them to speak;
    but let them be in subjection,

as the law also says.

1Co 14:35

If they desire to learn anything,
let them ask their own husbands at home,
for
it is shameful for a woman to chatter in the assembly.

1Co 14:36

What?
Was it from you that the word of God went out?
Or did it come to you alone?

1Co 14:37

If any man thinks himself to be a prophet, or spiritual,
let him recognize the things which I write to you,
that
they are the commandment of the Lord.

1Co 14:38

But
if anyone is ignorant,
let him be ignorant.

1Co 14:39

Therefore,
brothers,
desire earnestly to prophesy,
and
don't forbid speaking with other languages.

1Co 14:40

Let all things be done decently and in order.

1 Corinthian Chapter 15

1Co 15:1

Now
I declare to you,
  brothers,
the Good News which I preached to you,
   which also you received,
   in which you also stand,

1Co 15:2

   by which also you are saved,
  if you hold firmly the word
  which I preached to you –
    unless you believed in vain.

1Co 15:3

For
I delivered to you
   first of all that which I also received:
1. that Christ died for our sins
   according to the Scriptures,

1Co 15:4

2. that he was buried,
3. that he was raised on the third day according to the Scriptures,

1Co 15:5

  and
4. that he appeared to Cephas,
   then to the twelve.

1Co 15:6

  Then he appeared to over five hundred brothers at once,
   most of whom remain until now,
   but some have also fallen asleep.

1Co 15:7

  Then he appeared to James,

then to all the apostles,

1Co 15:8

and   last of all,
  as to the child born at the wrong time,
he appeared to me also.

1Co 15:9

  For
  I am the least of the apostles,
   who is not worthy to be called an apostle,
  because
  I persecuted the assembly of God.

1Co 15:10

  But by the grace of God I am what I am.
   His grace which was bestowed on me was not futile,
   but I worked more than all of them;
   yet not I,
   but the grace of God which was with me.

1Co 15:11

  Whether then it is I or they,
so we preach,
and
so you believed.

1Co 15:12

 Now
if Christ is preached,
that he has been raised from the dead,
how do some among you say that there is no resurrection of the dead?

1Co 15:13

 a But if there is no resurrection of the dead,
  neither has Christ been raised.

1Co 15:14

 b If Christ has not been raised,
  then our preaching is in vain,

and
your faith also is in vain.

1Co 15:15

Yes,
we are found false witnesses of God,
  because we testified about God that he raised up Christ,
  whom he didn't raise up,
  if it is so that the dead are not raised.

1Co 15:16

For if the dead aren't raised,
neither has Christ been raised.

1Co 15:17

If Christ has not been raised,
{a} your faith is vain;
  you are still in your sins.

1Co 15:18

{b} Then they also who are fallen asleep in Christ have perished.

1Co 15:19

If we have only hoped in Christ in this life,
  we are of all men most pitiable.

1Co 15:20

But now Christ has been raised from the dead.
He became the first fruits of those who are asleep.

1Co 15:21

For since
death came by man,
the resurrection of the dead also came by man.

1Co 15:22

For as
in Adam all die,
so also in Christ all will be made alive.

1Co 15:23

But each in his own order:
  1 Christ the first fruits,

2 then those who are Christ's,
  at his coming.

1Co 15:24

3 Then the end comes,
   when he will deliver up the Kingdom to God, even the Father;
   when he will have abolished
          all rule   and
          all authority   and
            power.

1Co 15:25

  For
  he must reign
    until he has put all his enemies under his feet.

1Co 15:26

  The last enemy that will be abolished is death.

1Co 15:27

   For,
  "He put all things in subjection under his feet."
            [Psalm 8:6]
  But when he says,
  "All things are put in subjection,"
  it is evident that he is excepted
     who subjected all things to him.

1Co 15:28

4. When all things have been subjected to him,
   then the Son will also himself be subjected to him
     who subjected all things to him,
   that
   God may be all in all.

1Co 15:29

Or else
Q1 what will they do who are baptized for the dead?
Q2 If the dead aren't raised at all,
  why then are they baptized for the dead?

Q3 Why do we also stand in jeopardy every hour?

  I affirm,
    by the boasting in you
      which I have in Christ Jesus our Lord,
  I die daily.

Q4 If I fought with animals at Ephesus for human purposes,
  what does it profit me?
If the dead are not raised,
then
"let us eat and drink,
for tomorrow we die."   [Isaiah 22:13]

  1. Don't be deceived!
    "Evil companionships corrupt good morals."

  2. Wake up righteously,
   and
   don't sin,
    for some have no knowledge of God.
     I say this to your shame.

But
someone will say,
  a "How are the dead raised?"   and,
  b "With what kind of body do they come?"

  You foolish one,
  1. that which you yourself sow is not made alive unless it dies.

  2. That which you sow, you don't sow the body that will be,
   but a bare grain,

maybe of wheat,
or of some other kind.

1Co 15:38

But
God gives it a body   even as it pleased him,
and to each seed a body of its own.

1Co 15:39

All flesh is not the same flesh,
but there is one flesh of men,
another flesh of animals,
another of fish,
and another of birds.

1Co 15:40

There are also celestial bodies,
and terrestrial bodies;
but the glory of the celestial differs from that of the terrestrial.

1Co 15:41

There is one glory of the sun,
another glory of the moon,
and another glory of the stars;
for one star differs from another star in glory.

1Co 15:42

So also is the resurrection of the dead.
It is sown in corruption; it is raised in incorruption.

1Co 15:43

It is sown in dishonor; it is raised in glory.
It is sown in weakness; it is raised in power.

1Co 15:44

It is sown a natural body; it is raised a spiritual body.
There is a natural body and there is also a spiritual body.

1Co 15:45

So also it is written,
"The first man, Adam, became a living soul."   [Genesis 2:7]
The last Adam became a life-giving spirit.

However
that which is spiritual isn't first,
but that which is natural,
then that which is spiritual.

The first man is of the earth,   made of dust.
The second man is the Lord from heaven.

  As is the one made of dust, such are those who are also made of
dust;
  and
  as is the heavenly, such are they also that are heavenly.

As we have borne the image of those made of dust,
let's also bear the image of the heavenly.
        [NU, TR read "we will" instead of "let's"]

  Now
I say this,
  brothers,
that
1. flesh and blood can't inherit the Kingdom of God;
2. neither does corruption inherit incorruption.

  Behold,
  I tell you a mystery.
We will not all sleep,
but
we will all be changed,

  in a moment,
  in the twinkling of an eye,
  at the last trumpet.

For
  the trumpet will sound,   and
  the dead will be raised incorruptible,   and
  we will be changed.

1Co 15:53

For
  this corruptible must put on incorruption,   and
  this mortal must put on immortality.

1Co 15:54

But
  1 when this corruptible will have put on incorruption, and
     this mortal will have put on immortality,
  2 then what is written will happen:
   "Death is swallowed up in victory."   [Isaiah 25:8]

1Co 15:55

   "Death, where is your sting?
   Hades [or,Hell], where is your victory?" [Hosea 13:14]

1Co 15:56

   The sting of death is sin,   and
   the power of sin is the law.

1Co 15:57

   But thanks be to God,
    who gives us the victory
     through our Lord Jesus Christ.

1Co 15:58

  Therefore,
 my beloved brothers,
1 be steadfast,
2 immovable,
3always abounding in the Lord's work,
 because
 you know that your labor is not in vain in the Lord.

1 Corinthian Chapter 16

1Co 16:1

Now
concerning the collection for the saints,
  as I commanded the assemblies of Galatia,
  you do likewise.

1Co 16:2

  On the first day of the week,
let each one of you save,
    as he may prosper,
  that
  no collections be made when I come.

1Co 16:3

When I arrive,
  I will send
    whoever you approve
      with letters
       to carry your gracious gift to Jerusalem.

1Co 16:4

  If it is appropriate for me to go also,
    they will go with me.

1Co 16:5

  But
I will come to you
  when I have passed through Macedonia,
  for I am passing through Macedonia.

1Co 16:6

But with you it may be that I will stay,
  or even winter,
that you may send me on my journey wherever I go.

1Co 16:7

  For I do not wish to see you now in passing,

but I hope to stay a while with you,
　if the Lord permits.

1Co 16:8

But I will stay at Ephesus until Pentecost,

1Co 16:9

　for a great and effective door has opened to me,
　and
　there are many adversaries.

1Co 16:10

Now
[1] if Timothy comes,
　　see that he is with you without fear,
　for he does the work of the Lord,
　as I also do.

1Co 16:11

　Therefore
　let no one despise him.
　But set him forward on his journey in peace,
　　that he may come to me;
　　for I expect him with the brothers.

1Co 16:12

Now
[2] concerning Apollos,
　　　the brother,
　　I strongly urged him to come to you with the brothers;
　　and it was not at all his desire to come now;
　but he will come when he has an opportunity.

1Co 16:13

Watch!
Stand firm in the faith!
Be courageous!
Be strong!

1Co 16:14

Let all that you do be done in love.

Now
1Co 16:15
[3] I beg you,
  brothers
  (you know the house of Stephanas,
    that it is the first fruits of Achaia,   and
    that they have set themselves to serve the saints),

1Co 16:16
  that you also be in subjection to such,
    and to everyone who helps in the work and labors.

1Co 16:17
  I rejoice at the coming of
    Stephanas,
    Fortunatus,   and
    Achaicus;
  for that which was lacking on your part, they supplied.

1Co 16:18
  For they refreshed my spirit and yours.
Therefore
acknowledge those who are like that.

1Co 16:19
The assemblies of Asia greet you.
Aquila and Priscilla greet you much in the Lord,
  together with the assembly that is in their house.

1Co 16:20
All the brothers greet you.
Greet one another with a holy kiss.

1Co 16:21
This greeting is by me, Paul,
  with my own hand.

1Co 16:22
If any man doesn't love the Lord Jesus Christ,
let him be accursed   [Greek: anathema.].

Come, Lord!   [Aramaic: Maranatha!]

1Co 16:23

The grace of the Lord Jesus Christ be with you.

1Co 16:24

My love to all of you in Christ Jesus.
Amen.

< The End of the First Letter to the Corinthians >

Contact us at: kindlepub47@gmail.com
Website: http://www.LearnPianoWithRosa.com/

Outline of The Second Letter of Paul to the Corinthians

1. Introduction (1:1–11)

2. Minister & Ministry (1:12-7)
    A. Ministry of the New Covenant (1:12-3)
    B. Treasures in Clay Jars (4)
    C. Ministry of Reconciliation (5)
    D. God's Fellow Worker (6-7)

3. Collection for Jerusalem Church (8-9)

4. Apostolic Authority (10-13:10)
    A. Paul's Defense of his Ministry (10)
    B. False Apostles (11)
    C. Paul's Thorn (12)
    D. Final Warnings (13:1-10)

5. Final Greetings (13:11-14)

2 Corinthians Chapter 1

2Co 1:1

Paul,
    an apostle of Christ Jesus
        through the will of God,
and
Timothy
    our brother,
to the assembly of God
        which is at Corinth,
    with all the saints
        who are in the whole of Achaia:

2Co 1:2

Grace
    to you
and
peace
    from God our Father   and
        the Lord Jesus Christ.

2Co 1:3

Blessed be the   God   and
                Father
                    of our Lord Jesus Christ,
          the   Father of mercies   and
                God of all comfort;

2Co 1:4

who
    comforts us in all our affliction,
    that
    we may be able to comfort those who are in any affliction,

through the comfort with which we ourselves are
comforted
by God.

2Co 1:5

For
as the sufferings of Christ abound to us,
even so
our comfort also abounds
through Christ.

2Co 1:6

1.   But if we are afflicted, it is for your comfort and salvation.
2.   If we are comforted,   it is for your comfort,
which produces in you the patient
enduring of the same sufferings
which we also suffer.

2Co 1:7

Our hope for you is steadfast,
knowing that,
since you are partakers   of the sufferings,
so also are you   of the comfort.

2Co 1:8

For
we don't desire to have you uninformed,
brothers,
concerning our affliction
which happened to us in Asia,
that
we were weighed down exceedingly,
beyond our power,
so much that
we despaired even of life.

2Co 1:9

Yes,
we ourselves have had the sentence of death

within ourselves,
that
1. we should not trust in ourselves,
2. but in God
who raises the dead,

2Co 1:10

who   delivered us out of so great a death,
and
does deliver;
on whom
we have set our hope
that
he will also still deliver us;

2Co 1:11

you also helping together
on our behalf
by your supplication;
that,
for the gift bestowed on us
by means of many,
thanks may be given
by many persons on your behalf.

2Co 1:12

For
our boasting is this:
the testimony of our conscience,
that a. in holiness   and   sincerity of God,
b. not in fleshly wisdom   but   in the grace of God
we behaved   ourselves in the world,   and
more abundantly toward you.

2Co 1:13

For
we write
no other things to you,

than what you   read or even

acknowledge,

and

I hope you will acknowledge to the end;

2Co 1:14

as also you acknowledged us in part,

that

we are your boasting,

even as you also are ours,

in the day of our Lord Jesus.

2Co 1:15

In this confidence,

I was determined

1. to come first to you,

that

you might have a second benefit;

2Co 1:16

and

by you

2. to pass into Macedonia,

and again

3. from Macedonia to come to you,

and

4. to be sent forward

by you

on my journey to Judea.

2Co 1:17

Q1   When I therefore was thus determined,

did I show fickleness?

Or

Q2   the things that I purpose,

do I purpose

according to the flesh,

that

with me

there should be the "Yes, yes" and the "No, no?"

2Co 1:18

But

as God is faithful,

our word toward you was not "Yes and no."

2Co 1:19

For

the Son of God, Jesus Christ,

who was preached among you

by us,

by   me,

Silvanus,   and

Timothy,

was not "Yes and no,"

but

in him is "Yes."

2Co 1:20

For however

many are the promises of God,

in him

1. is the "Yes."

Therefore

also through him

2. is the "Amen,"

to the glory of God

through us.

2Co 1:21

Now

he

who   establishes us

with you in Christ,

and

anointed us,

is God;

2Co 1:22

who also   1. sealed us,   and
                                 2. gave us the down payment of the Spirit
                                           in our hearts.

2Co 1:23

But
I call God for a witness to my soul,
that
     1. I didn't come to Corinth to spare you.

2Co 1:24

     2. Not that we have lordship over your faith,
     3. but are fellow workers with you for your joy.
        For
        you stand firm in faith.

2 Corinthians Chapter 2

2Co 2:1

But I determined this for myself,
    that
I would not come to you again in sorrow.

2Co 2:2

For if I make you sorry,
then who will make me glad
but he who is made sorry by me?

2Co 2:3

And
I wrote this very thing to you,
        so that,
        when I came,
I wouldn't have sorrow
        from them of whom I ought to rejoice;
    having confidence in you all,
that
my joy would be shared by all of you.

2Co 2:4

For   out of much affliction   and
            anguish of heart
I wrote to you
        with many tears,
    a. not that you should be made sorry,
    b. but that you might know the love
                that I have so abundantly for you.

2Co 2:5

But
    if any has caused sorrow,
he has caused sorrow,

not to me,
    but   in part (that I not press too heavily)
    to you all.

2Co 2:6

Sufficient to such a one is this punishment
    which was inflicted by the many;

2Co 2:7

so that
        on the contrary
you should rather
        a. forgive him and
        b. comfort him,
    lest
        by any means
such a one should be swallowed up with his excessive sorrow.

2Co 2:8

    Therefore
I beg you
    to **confirm your love** toward him.

2Co 2:9

    For to this end
I also wrote,
that
I might know the proof of you,
        whether you are obedient in all things.

2Co 2:10

Now
I also forgive
        whomever you forgive anything.
    For
    if indeed I have forgiven anything,
    I have forgiven that one
        for your sakes
        in the presence of Christ,

that
no advantage may be gained over us by Satan;
    for
    we are not ignorant of his schemes.

    Now
    when I came to Troas
            for the Good News of Christ,
    and
    when a door was opened to me in the Lord,

I had no relief for my spirit,
    because
    I didn't find Titus,
                    my brother,
    but
            taking my leave of them,
    I went out into Macedonia.

    Now
thanks be to God,
    who always
    1. leads us in triumph in Christ,
            and
    2. reveals
                    through us
            the sweet aroma of his knowledge
                    in every place.

For
we are a sweet aroma of Christ to God,
    a. in those who are saved,   and
    b. in those who perish;

      a. to the one a stench from death to death;
      b. to the other a sweet aroma from life to life.
Who is sufficient for these things?

For
1. we are not as so many,
               peddling the word of God.
But
      as of sincerity,
      but
      as of God,
        in the sight of God,
2. we speak in Christ.

2 Corinthians Chapter 3

2Co 3:1

Are we beginning again to commend ourselves?
Or
do we need,

                as do some,
   letters of commendation to you   or
                             from you?

2Co 3:2

   You are our letter,
   1. written in our hearts,
   2. known   and
   3. read by all men;

2Co 3:3

   being revealed
       that
   you are a letter of Christ,
   served by us,
       written
   1. not with ink,
   2. but with the Spirit of the living God;
   3. not in tablets of stone,
   4. but in tablets that are hearts of flesh.

2Co 3:4

Such confidence we have through Christ toward God;

2Co 3:5

   not that we are sufficient of ourselves,
       to account anything as from ourselves;
   but our sufficiency is from God;

2Co 3:6

      who also made us sufficient

as servants of a new covenant;
1. not of the letter,
2. but of the Spirit.

For
the letter kills,
but the Spirit gives life.

2Co 3:7

But
(a) if the service of death,
written engraved on stones,
came with glory,
so that
the children of Israel could not look steadfastly on the face
of Moses
for the glory of his face;
which was passing away:

2Co 3:8

(b) won't service of the Spirit be with much more glory?

2Co 3:9

For
(a) if the service of condemnation has glory,
(b) the service of righteousness exceeds much more in glory.

2Co 3:10

For
most certainly
that which has been made glorious has not been made glorious
in this respect,
by reason of the glory that surpasses.

2Co 3:11

For
(a) if that which passes away was with glory,
(b) much more that which remains is in glory.

2Co 3:12

Having therefore such a hope,

we use great boldness of speech,

2Co 3:13

    and
not as Moses,
      who put a veil on his face,
      that
      the children of Israel wouldn't look steadfastly on
       the end of that which was passing away.

2Co 3:14

    But
their minds were hardened,
      for until this very day
        at the reading of the old covenant
      the same veil remains,
        because in Christ it passes away.

2Co 3:15

    But to this day,
      when Moses is read,
    a veil lies on their heart.

2Co 3:16

    But whenever one turns to the Lord,
    the veil is taken away.

2Co 3:17

Now
the Lord is the Spirit
and
    where the Spirit of the Lord is,
there is liberty.

2Co 3:18

    But
we all,
    with unveiled face
    beholding as in a mirror the glory of the Lord,
are transformed into the same image

from glory to glory,
even as from   the Lord,
    the Spirit.

2 Corinthians Chapter 4

2Co 4:1

Therefore seeing we have this ministry,
even as we obtained mercy,
we don't faint.

2Co 4:2

But
we have renounced the hidden things of shame,
not walking in craftiness,
nor handling the word of God deceitfully;
but by the manifestation of the truth
commending ourselves
to every man's conscience
in the sight of God.

2Co 4:3

Even
if our Good News is veiled,
it is veiled in those who perish;

2Co 4:4

in whom the god of this world has blinded the minds of the
unbelieving,
that
the light of the Good News of the glory of Christ,
who is the image of God,
should not dawn on them.

2Co 4:5

For
we don't preach (1) ourselves, but Christ Jesus as Lord,
and
(2) ourselves as your servants
for Jesus' sake;

seeing it is God who said,
"Light will shine out of darkness," [Genesis 1:3]
who has shone in our hearts,
to give the light of the knowledge of the glory of God
in the face of Jesus Christ.

But
we have this treasure in clay vessels,
that the exceeding greatness of the power may be of God,
and
not from ourselves.

We are
1. pressed on every side, yet not crushed;
2. perplexed, yet not to despair;

3. pursued, yet not forsaken;
4. struck down, yet not destroyed;

always carrying in the body
a. the putting to death of the Lord Jesus,
that
b. the life of Jesus may also be revealed in our body.

For
we
who live
are always delivered to death
for Jesus' sake,
that
the life also of Jesus may be revealed in our mortal flesh.

So then

a. death works in us,
but
b. life in you.

2Co 4:13

But
          having the same spirit of faith,
          according to that which is written,
     "I believed,
     and   therefore
     I spoke."   [Psalm 116:10]
We also believe,
and   therefore also
we speak;

2Co 4:14

     knowing that
he
          who raised the Lord Jesus
will raise us also with Jesus,
and
will present us with you.

2Co 4:15

     For
all things are for your sakes,
that
the grace,
          being multiplied
               through the many,
may cause the thanksgiving to abound
     to the glory of God.

2Co 4:16

     Therefore
we don't faint,
but
though our outward man is decaying,

yet our inward man is renewed day by day.

2Co 4:17

For our light affliction,
      which is for the moment,
works for us more and more exceedingly an eternal weight of glory;

2Co 4:18

  while
we don't look at the things which are seen,
but at the things which are not seen.
      For the things which are seen are temporal,
      but the things which are not seen are eternal.

2 Corinthians Chapter 5

2Co 5:1

For we know that if the earthly house of our tent is dissolved,
we have a building from God,
      a house
             a. not made with hands,
             b. eternal,
             c. in the heavens.

2Co 5:2

    For
    most certainly in this
we groan,
      longing to be clothed with our habitation
                which is from heaven;

2Co 5:3

        if so be that being clothed
      we will not be found naked.

2Co 5:4

    For indeed
we
      who are in this tent
do groan,
      being burdened;
not that we desire to be unclothed,
but that we desire to be clothed,
that
what is mortal may be swallowed up by life.

2Co 5:5

Now
he who made us for this very thing is God,
    who also gave to us the down payment of the Spirit.

Therefore,
we are always confident
    and
    know that
        while we are at home in the body,
        we are absent from the Lord;

for
we walk   (a) by faith,
          (b) not by sight.

We (1) are courageous,
                I say,
    and
    (2) are willing rather
    a. to be absent from the body,
        and
    b. to be at home with the Lord.

    Therefore also
we make it our aim,
        whether at home or absent,
to be well pleasing to him.

For
we must all be revealed before the judgment seat of Christ;
    that
    each one may receive the things in the body,
        according to what he has done,
          whether good or bad.

    Knowing therefore the fear of the Lord,
we persuade men,

but
a. we are revealed to God;
    and   I hope that
b. we are revealed also in your consciences.

2Co 5:12

For
we a. are not commending ourselves to you again,
      but
  b. speak

        as giving you occasion of boasting on our behalf,
        that
        you may have something to answer those
              who boast a. in appearance,   and
                       b. not in heart.

2Co 5:13

    For
1. if we are beside ourselves,   it is for God.
    Or
2. if we are of sober mind,   it is for you.

2Co 5:14

    For
the love of Christ constrains us;
    because
    we judge thus,
        that one died for all,
        therefore all died.

2Co 5:15

He died for all,
that
those who live should no longer live (1) to themselves,
    but (2) to him
        who for their sakes died and rose again.

2Co 5:16

    Therefore

we know no one after the flesh from now on.
 Even though we have known Christ after the flesh,
 yet now we know him so no more.

2Co 5:17

 Therefore
 if anyone is in Christ,
he is a new creation.
  a. The old things have passed away.
   Behold,
  b. all things have become new.

2Co 5:18

But
all things are of God,
 who 1. reconciled us to himself
     through Jesus Christ,
    and
   2. gave to us the ministry of reconciliation;

2Co 5:19

    namely,
   that
   God was
      in Christ
   1. reconciling the world to himself,
   2. not reckoning to them their trespasses,
     and
   3. having committed to us the word of
reconciliation.

2Co 5:20

We are therefore ambassadors
     on behalf of Christ,
  as though God were entreating by us:
we beg you
     on behalf of Christ,
  be reconciled to God.

For
     him   who knew no sin
he made to be sin
                  on our behalf;
so that
        in him
we might become the righteousness of God.

2 Corinthians Chapter 6

2Co 6:1

Working together,
we entreat also that you not receive the grace of God in vain,

2Co 6:2

for he says,
"At an acceptable time I listened to you,
in a day of salvation I helped you."

[Isaiah 49:8]

Behold,
now is the acceptable time.
Behold,
now is the day of salvation.

2Co 6:3

We give no occasion of stumbling in anything,
that
our service may not be blamed,

2Co 6:4

but in everything commending ourselves,
as servants of God,
1. in great endurance,
2. in afflictions,
3. in hardships,
4. in distresses,

2Co 6:5

5. in beatings,
6. in imprisonments,
7. in riots,
8. in labors,
9. in watchings,
10. in fastings;

2Co 6:6

11. in pureness,
12. in knowledge,
13. in patience,
14. in kindness,
15. in the Holy Spirit,
16. in sincere love,

2Co 6:7

17. in the word of truth,
18. in the power of God;
a. by the armor of righteousness
on the right hand   and
on the left,

2Co 6:8

b. by glory and dishonor,
c. by evil report and good report;
1. as deceivers, and yet true;

2Co 6:9

2. as unknown, and yet well known;
3. as dying, and behold, we live;
4. as punished, and not killed;

2Co 6:10

5. as sorrowful, yet always rejoicing;
6. as poor, yet making many rich;
7. as having nothing, and yet possessing all things.

2Co 6:11

Our mouth is open to you,
        Corinthians.
Our heart is enlarged.

2Co 6:12

You are not restricted by us,
but
you are restricted by your own affections.

2Co 6:13

    Now in return,

I speak as to my children,
you also be open wide.

2Co 6:14

Don't be unequally yoked with unbelievers,
for

1. what fellowship have righteousness and iniquity?   Or
2. what fellowship has light with darkness?

2Co 6:15

3. What agreement has Christ with Belial?   Or
4. what portion has a believer with an unbeliever?

2Co 6:16

5. What agreement has a temple of God with idols?

For
you are a temple of the living God.
Even as God said,
"I will dwell in them,   and walk in them;
and
I will be their God,   and they will be my people."

[Leviticus 26:12; Jeremiah 32:38; Ezekiel 37:27]

2Co 6:17

"Therefore,
1. 'Come out from among them,
and
2. be separate,'   says the Lord.
3. 'Touch no unclean thing.
I will receive you. '

[Isaiah 52:11; Ezekiel 20:34,41]

2Co 6:18

"I will be to you a Father.
You will be to me sons and daughters,'   says the Lord Almighty."

[2 Samuel 7:14; 7:8]

2 Corinthians Chapter 7

2Co 7:1

Having therefore these promises,
    beloved,

let us
1. cleanse ourselves from all defilement of flesh and spirit,
2. perfecting holiness in the fear of God.

2Co 7:2

Open your hearts to us.
We wronged no one.
We corrupted no one.
We took advantage of no one.

2Co 7:3

I say this not to condemn you,
    for I have said before,
    that
    you are in our hearts to   die together

                and
          live together.

2Co 7:4

Great is my boldness of speech toward you.
Great is my boasting on your behalf.
I am filled with comfort.
I overflow with joy in all our affliction.

2Co 7:5

    For even
when we had come into Macedonia,
our flesh had no relief,
but
we were afflicted on every side.
    Fightings were outside.

Fear was inside.

2Co 7:6

        Nevertheless,
     he who comforts the lowly,
God,
     comforted us by the coming of Titus;

2Co 7:7

     and
           not by his coming only,
     but also by the comfort with which he was comforted in you,
        while he told us of
                a. your longing,
                b. your mourning,
                    and
                c. your zeal for me;
     so that
     I rejoiced still more.

2Co 7:8

     For though
I made you sorry with my letter,
I do not regret it,
     though I did regret it.
     For
     I see that my letter made you sorry,
        though just for a while.

2Co 7:9

I now rejoice,
     not that you were made sorry,
     but that you were made sorry to repentance.
     For
you were made sorry in a godly way,
     that
you might suffer loss by us in nothing.

2Co 7:10

For
a. godly sorrow works repentance to salvation,
   which brings no regret.
But
b. the sorrow of the world works death.

2Co 7:11

For behold,
this same thing,
that
you were made sorry in a godly way,
   1. what earnest care it worked in you.
        Yes,
   2. what defense,
   3.   indignation,
   4.   fear,
   5.   longing,
   6.   zeal,   and
   7.   vengeance!
        In everything
you demonstrated yourselves to be pure in the matter.

2Co 7:12

So although I wrote to you,
I wrote
   a. not for his cause that did the wrong,
   b. nor for his cause that suffered the wrong,
        but that
   c. your earnest care for us might be revealed
        in you
        in the sight of God.

2Co 7:13

Therefore
we have been comforted.
   In our comfort
we rejoiced the more exceedingly

for the joy of Titus,
  because
  his spirit has been refreshed by you all.

2Co 7:14

For if in anything
I have boasted to him on your behalf,
I was not disappointed.
  But as we spoke all things to you in truth,
  so our glorying
              also which I made before Titus
  was found to be truth.

2Co 7:15

His affection is more abundantly toward you,
  while he remembers
    all of your obedience,
    how with fear and trembling you received him.

2Co 7:16

I rejoice
that
        in everything
I am confident concerning you.

2 Corinthians Chapter 8

2Co 8:1

Moreover,
brothers,
we make known to you the grace of God
which has been given in the assemblies of Macedonia;

2Co 8:2

how
that in much proof of affliction
the abundance of   their joy   and
their deep poverty
abounded to the riches of their liberality.

2Co 8:3

For
according to their power,
I testify,
yes and beyond their power,
they gave of their own accord,

2Co 8:4

begging us
with much entreaty
to receive this grace and the fellowship
in the service to the saints.

2Co 8:5

This was not as we had hoped,
but
first they gave their own selves (1) to the Lord,
and
(2) to us through the will of God.

2Co 8:6

So

we urged Titus,
that

      as he made a beginning before,
so he would also complete in you this grace.

2Co 8:7

      But
      as you abound in everything,
      1. in faith,
      2. utterance,
      3. knowledge,
      4. all earnestness,   and
      5. in your love to us,
   see that you also abound in this grace.

2Co 8:8

I speak not by way of commandment,
but
as proving

      through the earnestness of others
the sincerity also of your love.

2Co 8:9

      For you know the grace of our Lord Jesus Christ,
      that,

         though he was rich,
         yet for your sakes
      he became poor,
      that
      you

         through his poverty
      might become rich.

2Co 8:10

I give a judgment in this:
for this is expedient for you,
      who were the first to start a year ago,
         a. not only to do,

      b. but also to be willing.

2Co 8:11

But now complete the doing also,
that
as there was the readiness to be willing,
so there may be the completion also out of your ability.

2Co 8:12

For   if the readiness is there,
it is acceptable
      according to what you have,
      not according to what you don't have.

2Co 8:13

For
this is not that others may be eased and you distressed,

2Co 8:14

but for equality.
      Your abundance at this present time supplies their lack,
      that
      their abundance also may become a supply for your lack;
that there may be equality.

2Co 8:15

As it is written,
"He who gathered much had nothing left over,
and he who gathered little had no lack."   [Exodus
16:8]

2Co 8:16

But
thanks be to God,
      who puts the same earnest care for you
            into the heart of Titus.

2Co 8:17

For
he indeed accepted our exhortation,
      but being himself very earnest,

he went out to you of his own accord.

2Co 8:18

We have sent together with him
    the brother
        whose praise in the Good News is known
           through all the assemblies.

2Co 8:19

        Not only so,
      but who was also appointed by the assemblies
        to travel with us in this grace,
          which is served by us
             to the glory of the Lord himself,
          and to show our readiness.

2Co 8:20

We are avoiding this,
that
any man should blame us
        concerning this abundance which is administered by us.

2Co 8:21

Having regard for honorable things,
    a. not only in the sight of the Lord,
    b. but also in the sight of men.

2Co 8:22

We have sent with them our brother,
    whom we have many times proved earnest in many things,
    but now much more earnest,
    by reason of the great confidence which he has in you.

2Co 8:23

As for Titus,
    he is my partner and fellow worker for you.
As for our brothers,
    they are the apostles of the assemblies,
        the glory of Christ.

2Co 8:24

Therefore
show the proof (a) of your love to them in front of the assemblies,
and (b) of our boasting on your behalf.

2 Corinthians Chapter 9

2Co 9:1

It is indeed unnecessary for me to write to you
    concerning the service to the saints,

2Co 9:2

for
I know your readiness,
    of which I boast on your behalf to them of Macedonia,
        that
        Achaia has been prepared for a year past.
Your zeal has stirred up very many of them.

2Co 9:3

But
I have sent the brothers
    that
    our boasting
               on your behalf
    may not be in vain in this respect,
that,
        just as I said,
you may be prepared,

2Co 9:4

so that
I won't   by any means,
           if there come with me any of Macedonia
    and
    find you unprepared,
we (to say nothing of you) should be disappointed in this confident
boasting.

2Co 9:5

I thought it necessary therefore

to entreat the brothers
that
they would go before to you,
    and
arrange ahead of time the generous gift

                                        that you promised
before,
    that
    the same might be ready
        (a) as a matter of generosity,
        and
        (b) not of greediness.

                                        2Co 9:6

    Remember this:
he who sows sparingly will also reap sparingly.
He who sows bountifully will also reap bountifully.

                                        2Co 9:7

Let each man give
    (1) according as he has determined in his heart;
    (2) not grudgingly,
    (3) or under compulsion;
for
God loves a cheerful giver.

                                        2Co 9:8

And God is able to make all grace abound to you,
that
you,
        always having all sufficiency in everything,
may abound to every good work.

                                        2Co 9:9

    As it is written,
    "He has scattered abroad,
    he has given to the poor.
    His righteousness remains forever."   v[Psalm 112:9]

Now
may he
        who supplies (a) seed to the sower and
                (b) bread for food,
1. supply and multiply your seed for sowing,
and
2. increase the fruits of your righteousness;

you
      being enriched in everything
to all liberality,
    which works through us thanksgiving to God.

For
this service of giving
        that you perform
    not only makes up for lack among the saints,
    but abounds also through many givings of thanks to God;

      seeing that through the proof given by this service,
they glorify God
      for the obedience of your confession
          to the Good News of Christ,
    and
      for the liberality of your contribution to them and to
all;

      while
they themselves also,
    with supplication on your behalf,
yearn for you
      by reason of the exceeding grace of God in you.

Now
thanks be to God
    for his unspeakable gift!

2 Corinthians Chapter 10

2Co 10:1

Now
I Paul,
    myself,
entreat you
        by the humility and gentleness of Christ;
    I who in your presence am lowly among you,
    but being absent am bold toward you.

2Co 10:2

Yes,
I beg you
that
I may not,
    when present,
show courage with the confidence
        with which I intend to be bold against some,
           who consider us to be walking according to
the flesh.

2Co 10:3

For though we walk in the flesh,
we don't wage war
    according to the flesh;

2Co 10:4

for the weapons of our warfare are not of the flesh,
but mighty before God
    to the (1) throwing down of strongholds,

2Co 10:5

(2a) throwing down imaginations   and
(2b) every high thing

that is exalted against the
knowledge of God,
      and
      (3) bringing every thought into captivity to the
obedience of Christ;

2Co 10:6

      and
      (4) being in readiness to avenge all
disobedience,
          when your obedience will be
made full.

2Co 10:7

Do you look at things only as they appear in front of your face?
If anyone trusts in himself that he is Christ's,
let him consider this again with himself,
that,
      even as he is Christ's,
      so also we are Christ's.

2Co 10:8

      For though I should boast somewhat abundantly
         concerning our authority,
         (which the Lord gave for building you up,
         and not for casting you down)
I will not be disappointed,

2Co 10:9

that
I may not seem as if I desire to terrify you by my letters.

2Co 10:10

      For,
      "His letters," they say,
      "are weighty and strong,
      but his bodily presence is weak,
      and his speech is despised."

2Co 10:11

Let such a person consider this,
that what we are in word by letters when we are absent,
such are we also in deed when we are present.

2Co 10:12

For we are not bold to number   or
        compare ourselves with some of those who commend
themselves.
        But
        they themselves,
                measuring themselves by themselves,   and
                comparing themselves with themselves,
        are without understanding.

2Co 10:13

        But
we will not boast beyond proper limits,
but within the boundaries with which God appointed to us,
        which reach even to you.

2Co 10:14

For we don't stretch ourselves too much,
        as though we didn't reach to you.
        For we came even as far as to you with the Good News of
Christ,

2Co 10:15

        not boasting beyond proper limits in other men's labors,
but
        having hope that as your faith grows,
we will be abundantly enlarged by you
        in our sphere of influence,

2Co 10:16

        so as to preach the Good News even to the parts beyond you,
                not to boast in what someone else has already done.

2Co 10:17

        But
        "he who boasts,

let him boast in the Lord."   [Jeremiah 9:24]

2Co 10:18

For
it isn't he who commends himself
who is approved,
but whom the Lord commends.

2 Corinthians Chapter 11

2Co 11:1

I wish that you would bear with me in a little foolishness,
but indeed you do bear with me.

2Co 11:2

    For
I am jealous over you with a godly jealousy.
    For
I married you to one husband,
that
I might present you as a pure virgin to Christ.

2Co 11:3

    But
I am afraid that somehow,
        as the serpent deceived Eve in his craftiness,
so your minds might be corrupted from the simplicity that is in Christ.

2Co 11:4

    For (1) if he who comes preaches another Jesus,
        whom we did not preach,
or (2) if you receive a different spirit,
        which you did not receive,
or (3) a different "good news",
        which you did not accept,
you put up with that well enough.

2Co 11:5

    For
I reckon that I am not at all behind the very best apostles.

2Co 11:6

    But
though I am unskilled in speech,
yet I am not unskilled in knowledge.

No,
> in every way

we have been revealed to you in all things.

2Co 11:7

Or did I commit a sin in humbling myself that you might be exalted,
because I preached to you God's Good News free of charge?

2Co 11:8

I robbed other assemblies,
> taking wages from them

that I might serve you.

2Co 11:9

> When I was present with you and was in need,

I wasn't a burden on anyone,
>> for
>> the brothers,
>>> when they came from Macedonia,
>> supplied the measure of my need.
> In everything

I kept myself from being burdensome to you,
and
I will continue to do so.

2Co 11:10

As the truth of Christ is in me,
no one will stop me from this boasting in the regions of Achaia.

2Co 11:11

Why?
Because I don't love you?
God knows.

2Co 11:12

But what I do, that I will do,
that
I may cut off occasion
> from them that desire an occasion,
>> that in which they boast,

they may be found even as we.

2Co 11:13

For
such men are
     a. false apostles,
     b. deceitful workers,
     c. masquerading as Christ's apostles.

2Co 11:14

    And no wonder,
    for even
    Satan masquerades as an angel of light.

2Co 11:15

  It is no great thing therefore
  if his servants also masquerade as servants of
righteousness,
     whose end will be according to their works.

2Co 11:16

  I say again,
let no one think me foolish.
  But if so, yet receive me as foolish,
  that
I also may boast a little.

2Co 11:17

    That which I speak,
    I don't speak according to the Lord,
     but as in foolishness,
      in this confidence of boasting.

2Co 11:18

  Seeing that many boast after the flesh,
  I will also boast.

2Co 11:19

For
you bear with the foolish gladly,
  being wise.

For
you bear with a man,
- a. if he brings you into bondage,
- b. if he devours you,
- c. if he takes you captive,
- d. if he exalts himself,
- e. if he strikes you on the face.

I speak
by way of disparagement,
as though we had been weak.
Yet however any is bold (I speak in foolishness),
I am bold also.

- a. Are they Hebrews?   So am I.
- b. Are they Israelites?   So am I.
- c. Are they the seed of Abraham? So am I.

- d. Are they servants of Christ?
(I speak as one beside himself)

I am more so;
- 1. in labors more abundantly,
- 2. in prisons more abundantly,
- 3. in stripes above measure,
- 4. in deaths often.

- 5. Five times from the Jews I received forty stripes minus one.

- 6. Three times I was beaten with rods.
- 7. Once I was stoned.
- 8. Three times I suffered shipwreck.
- 9. I have been a night and a day in the deep.

10. I have been in travels often,
11. perils of rivers,
12. perils of robbers,
13. perils from my countrymen,
14. perils from the Gentiles,
15. perils in the city,
16. perils in the wilderness,
17. perils in the sea,
18. perils among false brothers;

2Co 11:27

19. in labor and travail,
20. in watchings often,
21. in hunger and thirst,
22. in fastings often,   and
23. in cold and nakedness.

2Co 11:28

Besides those things that are outside,
there is that which presses on me daily,
anxiety for all the assemblies.

2Co 11:29

Who is weak, and I am not weak?
Who is caused to stumble, and I don't burn with indignation?

2Co 11:30

If I must boast, I will boast of the things that concern my weakness.

2Co 11:31

The   God   and
          Father of the Lord Jesus Christ,
                    he who is blessed forevermore,
knows that I don't lie.

2Co 11:32

   In Damascus
the governor
          under King Aretas

guarded the city of the Damascenes desiring to arrest me.

2Co 11:33

   Through a window
I   was let down in a basket by the wall,
   and
   escaped his hands.

2 Corinthians Chapter 12

It is doubtless not profitable for me to boast.
    For
    I will come to visions and revelations of the Lord.

I know a man in Christ,
    fourteen years ago
        (whether in the body, I don't know,
        or whether out of the body, I don't know;
        God knows),
such a one caught up into the third heaven.

I know such a man
        (whether in the body,
        or outside of the body, I don't know;
        God knows),

how he (a) was caught up into Paradise,
        and (b) heard unspeakable words,
            which it is not lawful for a man to utter.

    On behalf of such a one
I will boast,
but on my own behalf I will not boast,
        except in my weaknesses.

For if I would desire to boast,
        I will not be foolish;
        for
        I will speak the truth.

But I refrain,
so that
no man may think more of me than that which he (a) sees in
me,   or

        (b) hears from me.

2Co 12:7

By reason of the exceeding greatness of the revelations,
that
I should not be exalted excessively,
there was given to me a thorn in the flesh,
      a messenger of Satan to torment me,
that
I should not be exalted excessively.

2Co 12:8

Concerning this thing,
I begged the Lord three times that it might depart from me.

2Co 12:9

He has said to me,
"My grace is sufficient for you,
for my power is made perfect in weakness."
Most gladly therefore I will rather glory in my weaknesses,
that
the power of Christ may rest on me.

2Co 12:10

Therefore
I take pleasure
    1. in weaknesses,
    2. in injuries,
    3. in necessities,
    4. in persecutions,
    5. in distresses,
        for Christ's sake.
For

when I am weak, then am I strong.

2Co 12:11

I have become foolish in boasting.
    You compelled me,
        for I ought to have been commended by you,
        for in nothing was I inferior to the very best apostles,
            though I am nothing.

2Co 12:12

Truly the signs of an apostle were worked among you
        in all patience,
        in signs and wonders and mighty works.

2Co 12:13

For what is there in which you were made inferior to the rest of the assemblies,
unless it is that I myself was not a burden to you?
            Forgive me this wrong.

2Co 12:14

        Behold,
this is the third time I am ready to come to you,
and
I will not be a burden to you;
for I seek   (a) not your possessions,
                    (b) but you.
        For
        the children ought not to save up for the parents,
        but
        the parents for the children.

2Co 12:15

I will most gladly spend and be spent for your souls.
        If I love you more abundantly,
        am I loved the less?

2Co 12:16

        But be it so,
        I did not myself burden you.

But,
        being crafty,
   I caught you with deception.

2Co 12:17

Q1. Did I take advantage of you by anyone of them whom I have sent to you?

2Co 12:18

       I exhorted Titus,
          and
       I sent the brother with him.

Q2. Did Titus take any advantage of you?
Q3. Didn't we walk in the same spirit?
Q4. Didn't we walk in the same steps?

2Co 12:19

     Again,

Q5. do you think that we are excusing ourselves to you?

   In the sight of God
we speak in Christ.
   But
all things,
       beloved,
are for your edifying.

2Co 12:20

For
I am afraid that by any means,
     when I come,
1. I might find you not the way I want to,
and
2. that I might be found by you as you don't desire;
3. that by any means there would be
     a. strife,
     b. jealousy,
     c. outbursts of anger,

        d. factions,
        e. slander,
        f. whisperings,
        g. proud thoughts,
        h. riots;

2Co 12:21

that
            again when I come
4. my God would humble me before you,
        and
        I would mourn for many of those
                who have (A) sinned before now,   and
                    (B) not repented of the
                                a. uncleanness   and
                                b. sexual immorality   and
                                c. lustfulness
                    which they committed.

2 Corinthians Chapter 13

2Co 13:1

This is the third time I am coming to you.
    "At the mouth of two or three witnesses shall every word be
established." [Deuteronomy 19:15]

2Co 13:2

        I have said beforehand,
        and
        I do say beforehand,
            as when I was present the second time,
    so now,
          being absent,
I write
    a. to those who have sinned before now,
        and
    b. to all the rest,
that,
        if I come again,
I will not spare;

2Co 13:3

    seeing that
you seek a proof of Christ
        who speaks in me;
        who toward you is not weak,
          but is powerful in you.

2Co 13:4

    For
he was crucified through weakness,
    yet he lives   through the power of God.
    For
we also are weak in him,

but we will live with him   through the power of God
                               toward you.

2Co 13:5

Test your own selves,
        whether you are in the faith.
Test your own selves.
Or don't you know
            as to your own selves,
that
Jesus Christ is in you?
        -- unless indeed you are disqualified.

2Co 13:6

    But I hope that you will know that we aren't disqualified.

2Co 13:7

Now
I pray to God that you do no evil;
    a. not that we may appear approved,
    b. but that you may do that which is honorable,
        though we are as reprobate.

2Co 13:8

   For
we can (a) do nothing against the truth,
    but (b) for the truth.

2Co 13:9

   For
we rejoice
    when   we are weak   and
        you are strong.
   And
this we also pray for,
    even your perfecting.

2Co 13:10

   For this cause
I write these things while absent,

that I may not deal sharply when present,
    according to the authority
        which the Lord gave me
            a. for building up,   and
            b. not for tearing down.

2Co 13:11

    Finally,
brothers,
    1. rejoice.
    2. Be perfected,
    3. be comforted,
    4. be of the same mind,
    5. live in peace,   and
the God of love and peace will be with you.

2Co 13:12

Greet one another with a holy kiss.

2Co 13:13

All the saints greet you.

2Co 13:14

A. The grace of the Lord Jesus Christ,
B. the love of God,   and
C. the fellowship of the Holy Spirit,
        be with you all.
Amen.

Printed in Great Britain
by Amazon

42720695R00093